NativeNorthwest.com • Vancouver, Canada • 604-266-9044 • info@nativenorthwest.com
Printed in Canada using soy-based inks and non-toxic coatings.
Paper sourced from sustainable forests.
ISBN 978-1-55476-205-7
First printing, April 2016. Second printing, May 2018. Third printing, February 2022.
Written by Melaney Gleeson-Lyall (Point), Musqueam and Snaw-naw-as, Coast Salish Nations
Layout by Jenny Poon
Partial proceeds from this publication support Indigenous learning programs.

ANIMALS

OF THE

Coast Salish First Nations and Native Art

Written by Melaney Gleeson-Lyall (Point)
Musqueam and Snaw-naw-as, Coast Salish Nations

Salish

SEA

The Salish Sea is the network of waterways located in the adjoining coastal areas of British Columbia and Washington. This ecological treasure is one of the world's largest and most biologically diverse inland seas. Its islands, estuaries, rivers and creeks are home to thousands of indigenous species of plants and animals, many of which are unique to this area.

The Salish Sea has a variety of different marine life animal species: 37 species of mammals, 172 species of birds, 247 species of fish and over 3000 species of invertebrates. There are 113 species listed as threatened or endangered.

Since time immemorial, this area has been inhabited by the Coast Salish people.

The rich culture of the Coast Salish has a deep-rooted connection to the land and water of the Pacific Northwest. This distinct and abundant eco system provides the Coast Salish people with sources of food, shelter, clothing and medicine, and is at the centre of their unique cultural beliefs and practices.

"The Coast Salish honour and respect the land's natural resources, including traditional foods such as salmon, clams and berries. The coastal forest animals, sea creatures and mountain dwellers are also integral to who we are as Salish people. Our history, myths, stories and art relate to the animals of the sky, land and water, and continue to form our living culture."
- Melaney Gleeson-Lyall (Point), Musqueam and Snaw-naw-as, Coast Salish Nations

Contents

Contributing Coast Salish Artists:

The following artists have been generous in sharing their culture, art and insights on their special relationships with the natural and supernatural world.

Did You Know?
Eagles are seen year round across the Salish Sea region. They rest in tree tops and swoop down to the water to hunt for fish, their primary food source. Eagles live in huge nests made of sticks built at the tops of tall trees. Their eyesight is 4-8 times sharper than a human's.

Eagle

Eagles fly highest in the sky and are closest to the Creator. They are prayer messengers. **They represent balance, strength, vision, honour and spirituality.**

Thunderbird

Thunderbirds are powerful, supernatural beings that bring strong winds, thunder and lightning. **They are the protectors of our people.**

Did You Know? There are stories about Thunderbirds so huge that they could carry whales in their talons.

Raven

Ravens are bringers of light.
They symbolize humour, cleverness and intelligence.

Did You Know?
Ravens are very smart and playful birds. They have been known to play with other animals, solve problems and have even been taught to count. Ravens can also imitate a variety of sounds, including the human voice.

Did You Know?
Hawks can see 8 times more clearly than humans and are one of the most intelligent birds.

Hawk

Hawks have great vision and concentration. **They are spirit helpers that bring guidance and focus to life.**

Did You Know?
Geese normally fly in formation, taking turns flying in the lead with the rest of the flock following behind in a v-shape. Geese use both body language and honking sounds to communicate with each other, and goslings even start to communicate with their parents while they're still in the egg.

Goose

Geese are silly and funny. They love family and always work as a team. **They symbolize determination, faithfulness and loyalty.**

Owl

Owls are messengers of change and guides to the spirit world.
They are keepers of sacred knowledge.

Did You Know?
The Great Horned Owl
is the most common owl
in the Pacific Northwest.
Owls have special feathers that
make them almost silent in flight.
Owls are more active at night,
and with their superior vision
can detect prey from
great distances.

Seagull & Starfish

Seagulls teach us not to be wasteful.
They are very chatty and like to be in community.
Starfish teach us about healing and renewal.

Did You Know?
The Glaucous-winged Gull is the most common gull around the Salish Sea. Gulls can drink both fresh and salt water. They have a special pair of glands right above their eyes which help to flush out the salt from their system.

Did You Know?
More starfish (or sea stars) are found along the Northwest Coast than anywhere else in the world. Most have 5 arms. If one breaks off, a new one will grow in its place.

Heron

Herons are resourceful, determined and graceful.
They nest in community.
They signify patience and tranquility.

Did You Know?
Herons nest in colonies.
One of the largest colonies
recorded was located near
Seattle, Washington, where
there were approximately 135
active nests. The Great Blue
Heron can swallow a fish
many times wider than
its narrow neck.

Hummingbirds

Hummingbirds are messengers of hope.
They are travellers of great distances.
They symbolize devotion, joy and agility.

Did You Know?
Butterflies have four wings and taste with their feet. Most butterflies feed on nectar from flowers.

Butterfly

Butterflies change through the stages of their lives.
They symbolize beauty, gentleness and harmony.

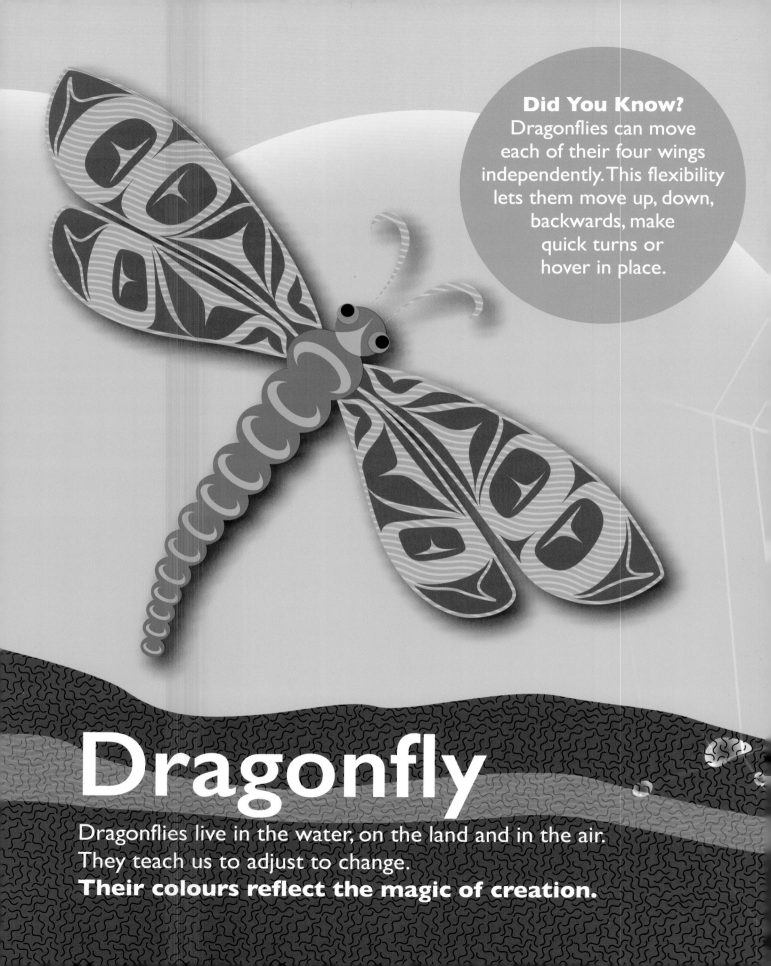

Dragonfly

Dragonflies live in the water, on the land and in the air.
They teach us to adjust to change.
Their colours reflect the magic of creation.

Spider

**Spiders teach us
the art of weaving.**

Did You Know?
Spiders have 8 legs
and most have 8 eyes.
Many spiders make
new webs everyday.

Frog

Frogs are messengers. To the Salish people, the croaking choruses of the frogs signal the end of winter and the arrival of spring. **They are the symbol of renewal and abundance.**

Did You Know?
Frogs usually live in small, quiet pools, swamps or ponds. Many frogs can jump 20 times their own height. They don't drink water with their mouths; they "drink" by absorbing water through their skin.

Did You Know?
Western Pond Turtles were
once the only species of
turtles in the ponds, lakes and
tributary waters of the Salish Sea.
Declared endangered, they are
slowly increasing their population
through support by recovery
programs in the Pacific Northwest.

Turtle

**Turtles teach us to
live life with perseverance
at a steady pace.**
They take the time to enjoy life.

Deer

Deer teach us to be gentle and kind with one another.
They are sensitive and always alert.

Did You Know?
Male deer grow new antlers every year and are called 'bucks' or 'stags'. Female deer are called 'does', and a group of deer is called a 'herd'. Most deer are born with white spots but lose them within a year.

Sasquatch

Sasquatch are supernatural beings and protectors of the forests.
They are the best at playing hide and seek!

Did You Know?
Sightings of Sasquatch (also known as Bigfoot) have been reported for thousands of years.

Bear & Bee

Bears teach us to find food and fish.
They represent protection, strength and bravery.

Bees love community and hard work.
They are very social and like to dance!
Bees make honey which is used for food and healing creams.

Did You Know?
Bears are omnivorous. They eat plants, berries and love salmon. Most species of bears hibernate in the winter, sometimes for up to seven months, and don't even wake up to eat. A bear can smell food, a mate, cubs or danger from far away.

Wolf

Wolves are communicators.
They are intelligent, powerful and playful.
They symbolize loyalty and strength.

Did You Know?
The Salish Sea is home to the Dungeness Crab, a traditional food for the Salish people renowned for its taste. Crabs live up to 3 years. They periodically shed their shells and can grow back their claws and legs.

Crab

Crabs walk sideways, teaching us that we need to find our own direction. **With their hard shells, crabs remind us of the need to protect ourselves and others.**

Rock Cod

Rock Cod are prehistoric-looking fish bringing ancient wisdom.

Did You Know?
The Salish Sea has 25 species of rockfish. Each varies in their lifespan. The Rougheye Rockfish can live up to 200 years. Rockfish give birth to live young rather than eggs. The babies are born tail first, and arrive in groups of around 40 at a time.

Sturgeon

The White Sturgeon is found in the sto:lo, known as the Fraser River.
They were mainstays of our traditional diet.
Sturgeon have survived through generations and represent longevity and resilience.
Sturgeon are the guardians of the river.

Did You Know?
Sturgeon can live up to 150 years, can grow to over 6 meters in length and weigh up to 816 kg.

Octopus

Octopuses are magical. They are intelligent, mysterious and flexible. They can change their shapes and are masters of disguise.

Did You Know?
The Giant Pacific Octopus grows larger and lives longer than any other octopus. They can reach sizes in excess of 45 kg. This octopus can grow to over 5 meters, lives in deep and shallow water and can live up to 5 years.

Salmon

Salmon are vital to our Coast Salish life and traditions. **They represent life and sustenance.** A first salmon ceremony is celebrated to honour the returning salmon every year.

Did You Know?
Chinook, also known as king salmon, are the largest of the five Pacific salmon species, which also include coho (silver), chum (dog), pink (humpy), and sockeye (red). Salmon migrate from freshwater streams, lakes and rivers to salt water, and then back again to spawn.

Did You Know?
Pacific Harbor Seals are the most common marine mammal seen in the Salish Sea. They often lie on rocks during low tide. They can dive as deep as 128 m and can stay under water as long as 28 minutes.

Seal

Seals are curious creatures. They are shapeshifters as they swim through the waters. **They are a sign of abundance.**

Dogfish Shark

The dogfish sharks were so abundant they could be grabbed by hand from the canoes. Their rough skins were dried and used as leather and sand paper to smooth the canoes. **The shark represents grace, power and instinct.**

Did You Know?

Sharks need to move all the time because they don't have a swim bladder. Females may reach a length of 120 cm and weigh 6.3–9 kg; males are smaller. These sharks are called dogfish because they feed in packs and their young are called pups.

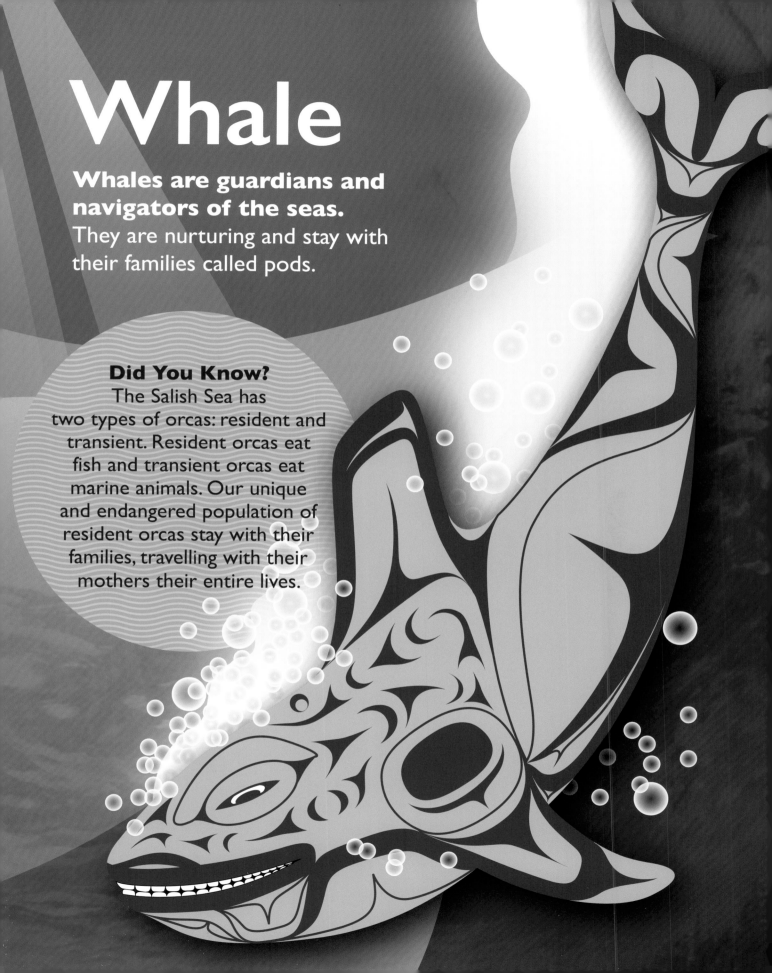

Whale

Whales are guardians and navigators of the seas.
They are nurturing and stay with their families called pods.

Did You Know?
The Salish Sea has two types of orcas: resident and transient. Resident orcas eat fish and transient orcas eat marine animals. Our unique and endangered population of resident orcas stay with their families, travelling with their mothers their entire lives.